LOOKING THRO' WINDOWS

PARADISE SQUARE

SQUARE

SHEFFIELD

Albert Jackson

Illustrated by Dennis Dalby

Albert Jackson

A popular local historian with a passion for expressing Sheffield's past and campaigning against redevelopment vandals.

Although not born in Sheffield, his residence over the last 30 years more than qualifies his acceptance by the City.

His first book, back in 2001, was a descriptive walk along The Sheffield & Tinsley Canal, and has been followed by historic walks around Sheffield and many an informative pub brochure.

Several publications as the 'Burngreave Cemetery Gravedigger' have been penned for the Friends of Burngreave Chapel and Cemetery.

albertjackson@hotmail.co.uk

Dennis Dalby

Artist Dennis Dalby began a career spanning over 50 years after winning a National Schools art competition at the age of 13 years.

Self taught, he is recognised as the 'Beermat artist', accepting commissions to illustrate beerclips for local Independent Breweries, but cannot resist recording life on beer mats whilst indulging his other favourite pastime.

Working in pen, graphite and oils, his work has a unique reflection on reality, while exposing a lighter, humorous edge.

e-mail: beermatartist@yahoo.com

CONTENTS

© 2008 – *Albert Jackson*
John Harley Publishing
Sheffield
any information or comments may be sent to…

albertjackson@hotmail.co.uk

ISBN 1-904185-01-0

Printed in Sheffield, Great Britain

Acknowledgements

The author would like to thank all those who have given their help and assistance in the research of this publication and in particular the staff of The Local Studies Library and Archives, His Grace the Duke of Norfolk's Surveyor, Terry Gorman, the many solicitors and their staff, and the all the others whose information, photographs and documents were invaluable.

Every attempt has been made to correctly portray the events mentioned in this publication; any errors or omissions are regretted.

The Hospital of Gilbert, Earl of Shrewsbury at Sheffield

In an extract from the will of Gilbert Earl of Shrewsbury – signed 4th May 1616, he leaves the following gift…

" I will and appoint an Hospitall bee founded at Sheffield, for perpetuall maintenance of twenty poore persons and to be called the Hospitall of Gilbert Earle of Shrewsbury and the same to be endowed with such revenues and possessions as my Executors shall think fit not being under two hundred pounds a yeare"

This then is the beginning of the story of Paradise Square. The will of Gilbert Earl of Shrewsbury was the origin of what today is 'The Shrewsbury Hospital Trust', set up to provide the revenue for the *Hospitall* and Alms Houses that today proudly dominate Norfolk Road opposite the Cholera Memorial.

Gilbert Talbot was born on 20th November 1553, he married at the age of 14 years to Mary Cavendish, and her mother was Bess of Hardwick. His elder brother Francis died childless leaving Gilbert as heir to the Talbot estate and its interests in Sheffield.

At the time of Gilbert's death in 1616, the estate was unable to fulfil the obligation due to the outcome of the Civil War and it was fifty years until the bequest could be satisfied with the building of the first hospital for 10 men and 10 women on what is now the site of the Park Square roundabout and opened in 1673.

Heavy flooding of the River Sheaf in November 1768 engulfed Sheffield; this caused severe damage to the Hospital with five pensioners drowned. Re-building took place and a Chapel added.

By 1823 the site had become over-developed and attractive for redevelopment so the decision was made to re-locate to the present site on Norfolk Road, where the Hospital, along with 35 Almshouses, a Chapel and houses for the Chaplain and a nurse were provided.

By an Act of Parliament made in 1725, the Hospital was to be administered by Trustees and an Agent and Receiver appointed by the Duke of Norfolk, this remains the case today in the form of the Shrewsbury Hospital Trust.

Revenue for the Trust benefits from ground rents on land, much of which is in the Sheffield City Centre and amongst this land is the land and buildings that are now known as Paradise Square.

There is an exception to this statement however, many of the Town Trustees were tenants of the Square but had as they had prospered had moved their residences outside the City boundaries thus losing their Sheffield Council vote.

An impromptu meeting was held and the outcome was the purchase of the Freehold by the Town Trustees of the centre of the Square from the Shrewsbury Hospital Trust and converting it into 39 car parking spaces to be let back to members thus qualifying them to a vote.

The original five houses on the east side of the Square (Numbers 4 – 12), built in 1736, by Joseph Broadbent, are the subject of a five hundred year lease at a ground rent of £1 each per year, however the remainder of the Square, which was built by his son in 1771, was the subject of a 99 year lease in 1776, which was backdated to 1771, and having matured, the property passed to the Hospital Trust, which now receives a market price for its revenue.

As successive Dukes have enlarged the Hospital site by building Almshouses and Sheltered Accommodation, thus furthering the Trust's objectives.

Bases upon information given by Nicholas Robinson; Surveyor to the Shrewsbury Hospital Trust.

Chapter One

Paradise Square

Paradise Square is the Hidden Gem in the heart of the Sheffield City Centre, tucked neatly behind the Cathedral it has mirrored the social and economic climate of the City and today stands proudly recording the history and changes that have brought today's prosperity, with its vision for the future.

The Square began life as an orchard, then a row of five houses built by a Sheffield merchant enclosing his estate. His son later took over the field and creating the square.

As Sheffield developed, the land around the Parish Church, which later was to become its Anglican Cathedral, was encroached for housing and commercial use.

At this time, behind the Church were fields where corn grew and orchards produced their fruit. They stretched down to the river, where on the opposite bank the Castle nurseries had produced the fruit and vegetables served on its tables.

To get down to the river and its corn mill at Kelham Island, a path needed to be taken through Hick's Stile Field.

An old folk law tale is told when on a winter's day a lame worker was making his way down towards the corn mill, when struggling over the style, he made his way through Hick's Stile Field.

Hearing strange noises, he began to shudder with goose-pimples covering his whole body. Suddenly he was confronted by the *Bargast !*

The *Bargast*, a fierce, large strange black dog like *Bogart*, has fang like teeth and large saucer-like eyes and lives by the sides of fields and hedgerows.

Struggling, he began to run away but the Bargast was gaining ground on him. In desperation he threw away his crutches and ran faster and faster. Escaping its clutches he continued to run until he got home and recounted the tale to his wife.

He found a new way to town after then and never needed his crutches again.

There are many such tales around Sheffield, and although it is hard to believe their authenticity, their similarity gives such stories a strange aura.

The land around Sheffield had over generations passed down from Earl Waltheof, Lord of Hallam and son of Siward the Strong – the Danish Earl of Northumberland. His Aula (hall) has yet to be located, but is believed to be on the site of the later Sheffield Castles. Waltheof was beheaded by William the Conqueror in 1076, for two acts of treason, and his body buried in the Abbey at Crowland.

William de Lovetot inherited his lands and built a wooden 'motte and bailey' castle. This castle was burned to the ground in 1266 after the line had passed to Thomas de Furnival.

The castle was rebuilt in 1270, the battlements constructed entirely of stone.

Mary, Queen of Scots was imprisoned in the castle between 1570 and 1584 by the Earl of Shrewsbury.

In his will, Gilbert, Earl of Shrewsbury, made provision for a hospital for the poor to be built and funded.

He died in 1616, when times were not good and it was some years later when the bequest was realised.

The castle was demolished by order of Parliament in 1648 after opting for the wrong side in the Civil War.

The Hospital of Gilbert, Earl of Shrewsbury at Sheffield was opened in 1673 on a site that now occupies the Park Square roundabout.

The funding for the Hospital and Alms Houses was provided by land set aside in trust to The Shrewsbury Hospital Trust and administered by His Grace the Duke of Norfolk.

The original hospital was flooded after the Sheaf burst its banks in 1768 ands after rebuilding, it was later sold then re-built and extended at its present site in 1823.

When the castle was demolished, then like now, the scrap men were not far away and all that could be sold, was sold.

Timber from the castle was bought by Thomas Hicks (Hick or Hycks). Hicks was a carpenter and took part in the building of the workhouse and many other local buildings. Doors, stone and fittings were also salvaged and used later.

Joseph Broadbent, a merchant who lived at the house opposite the Iris at Hartshead, took the land opposite Hick's Stile Field and built five houses, which then enclosed his garden.

These houses were taken on a five hundred year lease from the Hospital Trust and were known as Broadbent's Houses, although later they were referred to as Paradise Row.

The term 'Paradise' is the name given to enclosures close to a church.

Broadbent's son Thomas developed the Square around the other three sides of Hick's Stile Field, the centre of which was designed as a garden that was never achieved.

His lease of 1776 was a 99 year lease, reduced to 94 years as the Square had been built without permission five years earlier.

The three sides and Broadbent's Houses were named 'Paradise Square'.

The Square was a highly sought after development and attracted Solicitors, Doctors and wealthy Merchants who desired a Town address.

The population of Sheffield spiralled and housing was quickly knocked together. The areas from the Square, the Crofts, Scotland Street and Shalesmoor were built as slums and the Square and its beer houses attracted a new type of tenant.

The Stocks and the staff and steps of the Irish Cross were moved to the Square, the stocks used up to 1830 as a deterrent to drunkenness and blasphemy.

courtesy of Sheffield Local History Library
Pot dealer's house in the Square

The Pot Market, held outside the Town Hall (then next to the Cathedral) was moved into the Square at the instigation of the Police Constable around 1808.

The market gave cause to the Square being known as 'Pot Square', in addition to the stalls, the Square attracted china and pot dealers, cutlery and cooking utensil merchants to take premises.

The Pot Market is probably known more for the sale of wives as plates, cups and saucers. There were at least two women sold by their husbands in the market, the first for 6d (2½ pence) and a top of the range model for 5s.0d. (25 pence).

"In Sheffield market, I declare
'Tis true, upon my life,
A cotton spinner t'other day
By auction sold his wife.

Other tales from the market include the man who ate a cat for a bet and others even more unsavoury.

The Square was blessed with several pubs, The 'Q in the Corner' was known for the Blind Fiddlers. The Clown was of a lower class and remembered for its rats. Little is known of he Crown and the Clarence.

The Square went for over a year without a pub until in 2008 the Wig and Pen Bar and Restaurant extended from Campo Lane through the rear of Numbers 7/9 to restore the warmth and friendliness of a hostelry.

Number 18 Paradise Square had been built to incorporate the Masonic Hall on the upper floor. Access was by a stone staircase protruding into the Square with a balcony at the top.

This balcony was the rostrum for the speakers at meetings, many tens of thousand people have filled the Square to listen to Politicians, Clerics and Radical Reformists, mostly calmly yet some have caused riots and civil commotions.

Gas arrived in the Square in 1820 and with it the lighting. The Stump of the Cross had a lamp fitted on it until a permanent lamp was later fitted.

The gaslight post was the vantage point of the senior heckler at meetings, the crossbar of the lamp putting him level with the speaker.

courtesy of Sheffield Local History Library
Paradise Square and the Lamp

The Trustees of the Shrewsbury Hospital Trust were not happy with the direction that the Square was heading and made the decision to improve its image and regain its better reputation and clientele.

The staircase at number 18, was removed in 1889, as much to stop the public meetings as to remove its intrusion into the Square.

The door into the upper floor was transformed into a window frame, its Masonic architecture retained and enhancing the window.

Education Institutions played an important part in the Square. First was Hebblethwaite's Academy, which later became the Middle Class School. The Hebrew School was at Number 22.

The House of Help for Friendless Girls and Women occupied both Numbers 1 and 17/19. It gave the poor young girls instruction in skills to enable them to perform domestic duties.

Part of the Square was damaged by enemy action during the Sheffield Blitz in the Second World War and stress lines appeared in some of the buildings.

Following the Great War, several ex-servicemen's associations sprang up. One of these the National Federation of Disabled Sailors and Soldiers was at number 14. Many of these associations were to later join forces to become The Royal British Legion, who opened their 1st Branch in Lee Croft.

From the Roman Catholic parish of St Vincent, of the 960 men who answered the call to arms, only 253 returned. The Federation along with St Vincent's clergy held a Memorial Mass on Monday August 18th, 1919.

2,000 ex servicemen marched to the accompaniment of two Federation Bands from the Square around the town centre to a service at the Church.

At the conclusion of the service the Band played the Dead March from "Soul" and the "Last Post" was sounded by Bandsman Livesley.

The Town Trustees purchased the centre of the Square in the 1950's. The move was to protect the voting rights of the Town Trustees by leasing car parking spaces to them.

Repairs were hurriedly effected and then early in the 1960's major refurbishments were made to numbers 18 and 26, with the buildings gutted and rebuilt. The outsides were rebuilt in the original Georgian style, while the insides were reconstructed to the then modern standard.

The Square enjoys Grade II* listing being of "special architectural and historic interest", and this is strongly defended by the Shrewsbury Hospital Trust, The Sheffield Town Trust, Sheffield City Council and English Heritage, all of who preserve its appearance.

One night the Square was invaded by thieves who dug up and took away a number of paving stones. They were replaced within days by identical paving slabs taken from the pavement of the Corner Pin public house in Carlisle Street East.

In 2008, the long sought after door lanterns have been erected and illuminate the Square with a Victorian feel. The centre gas lamp is also to be replaced.

The gas supply reached the Square in 1820 and the head of the Irish Cross was converted into the first Gas Lamp to provide illumination.

Several of the down pipes outside the houses are cast with their dates, 1877 and 1787 and shown and indicate the length of time needed for the construction of the Square. There are also houses with the original mud scrapers outside the doors, others are repaired while others still have been removed and blocked in.

The Duke of Norfolk colours of blue and white are followed throughout the Square with blue doors and white paintwork, the exclusion to this is the "Broadbent's Buildings", where the paintwork is a contrasting black.

The Square is now close to perfection again and provides an attractive historic area in the centre of the City, standing still, the visitor can reflect on the happenings here over almost two and a half centuries past.

Chapter Two

The Bankers who built the Square

The beginning of the Square as we recognise it today, was by the courtesy of Joseph Broadbent, a merchant who had his home opposite the Iris at what is now Bank House.

In order to enclose his garden, Broadbent approached The Trustees of the Shrewsbury Hospital They prepared a Five hundred year lease for him to build five houses overlooking Hicks Stile Field.*

*The lease was signed on 10th February 1736 with a Ground Rent of £5 per annum.

The family home *Hartshead House* at Hartshead, had been built by Joseph's father Nicholas in 1728. The datestone has the legend...

B / N R / 1728

viz:

Broadbent /Nicholas, and his wife Rebecca/ built 1728

Joseph had seven children; sons Thomas and Joseph junior, and five daughters; Sarah, Ann, Susannah, Mary and Elizabeth.

It had been well planned in advance to cater for the many aspects of the Broadbent businesses, these included factoring for other Merchants.

In addition to the three storeys above ground plus an attic, it also had storeys of cellarways. Unique to the ground floor was a brick arched strongroom.

The elegance of the house was unique in its craftsmanship, which included ornate carved mantelpieces with overmantles.

It was believed that Joseph had built the houses for his daughters, but it transpires that after his death his last Will and Testament, in which the houses are referred to as *Broadbent's Buildings*, he bequeathed the following: -

To his wife Sarah and youngest daughter Elizabeth – One House.

A house each was bequeathed to younger son Joseph and to daughters Ann, Susannah and Mary.

His daughter Sarah had already been provided for. The rest of his estate and the family home; Hartshead House, was left to his son Thomas.

The original lease was sub-divided into five and the annual Ground Rent of £5 per annum became 5 x £1 per annum.

A survey was conducted for the Sheffield Water Company by William Fairbanks in September 1758, this showed the pipes laid between Town Head and Hartshead with branches into Paradise Row at its junction with Campo Lane and Virgin's Walk (St James' Row).

It shows Hick's Stile Field *still* opposite with no development to it and at the bottom of Paradise Row, a flight of steps falling eight feet six inches; connecting it to Workhouse Croft below.*

This row of five houses were much sought after in the 1750's by the local gentry which included Lawyers and Doctors.

At the end of the terrace, a footpath led through Wheat's Passage, passing through Wade's Orchard and Hartshead, then on towards the market at Castle Green.

The wealth and prestige of the Broadbent's grew and the two sons; Thomas and Joseph, prompted by other successes, opened a Bank at the family home of Hartshead House. Its entrance was by a door, still visible, at the side of the house beneath the arch at St. Peter's Close.

16

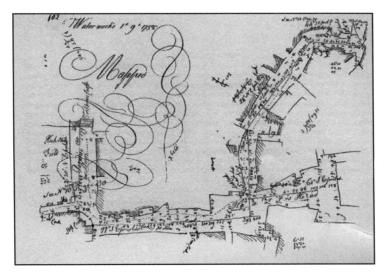

* Fairbanks waterworks survey

It was in 1771 that the Sheffield Bank was formed. This was also the year that Thomas Broadbent spoke unofficially to the Trustees office about his plans to develop the remaining three sides of Hick's Stile Field to form *Paradise Square*.

Development went ahead over the following years, although as discovered in 1776, no formal permission had been given, nor a lease obtained from the Trustees.

The remedy for this latter solution was the issuance of a 99 year lease, reduced to 94 years to compensate for the period that had already elapsed, but with no other penalty.

William Fairbanks conducted a survey again, this time between May 1771 and July 1776, where he outlined the construction of the site and the allocation of the plots being developed.*

It was in 1771 that the Sheffield Bank was formed, this was also the year that Thomas Broadbent spoke unofficially to the Trustees office about his plans to develop the remaining three sides of Hick's Stile Field to form *Paradise Square*.

Development went ahead over the following years, although as discovered in 1776, no formal permission had been given or a lease obtained from the Trustees.

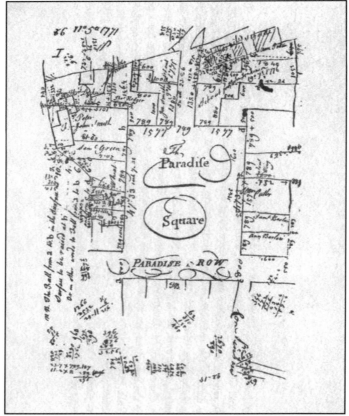

courtesy of Sheffield Local History Library
Fairbanks survey of Paradise Square

The survey identifies owners and tenants to include...

On one side of Silver Street Head was Joseph Smith, while on the other side it was for Jenkinson and Furniss.

The East side of the Square was the already existing Paradise Row belonging to T.B. (Thomas Broadbent) on the south side are the allotments for James Wheat, Samuel Green, Peter Smith and Thomas Duke; on the west, Thomas Rodger, Joseph Smith, William Jenkinson and Ann Potter, the north comprised Ann Barlow, Samuel Barlow, William Cutler and Samuel Wing.

Thus Paradise Square had been created to incorporate Paradise Row.

The early Ordnance Survey maps show the square to have a garden in the centre. This was never achieved, although a water pump was installed on the spot that now hosts the lamppost.

For a time the fortunes of the Broadbent's appeared to flourish, Thomas built for himself Page Hall.

The family home – Hartshead House, has had many names since it was built in 1728. Originally *Hartshead House*, it was to become *Broadbent House, Old Bankers House* and currently is *Bank House Chambers.*

While the development of the Square was coming along, dark clouds were forming above the *Sheffield Bank*.

A story is told of a Merchant; George Greaves arriving at the House on a Sunday in June 1782 requested Banking facilities. After being told that the Bank did not conduct business on a Sunday, he remonstrated and explained that he did not request any money, but wanted to deposit a large sum.

Not wishing to upset the Merchant further, the cash was accepted.

The following morning the Bank failed and trading was suspended.

There is no further mention of this unfortunate mans money, although after the collapse many customers sought to obtain satisfaction for their losses by various means.

Although only 21 years of age when he entered banking, Thomas Broadbent was a savage businessman and during his brief career had foreclosed on a prominent merchant and property owner; William Hildreth of Whitely Hall, Ecclesfield for a meagre £280 due on a Bond.

He was well known for operating this type of *hardfisted* practice and was often likened to the Dickens's character – Mr Josiah Boundary in *Hard Times* – A big loud man – The Bully of Humility.

It took over eighteen years to sort out the affairs of the Bank, which finally repaid thirteen shillings and a halfpence to creditors for every pound claimed (65p/£1).

After the collapse the family lost all their fortunes. The leases of the former Paradise Row and new Paradise Square were all sold and at Page Hall, James Milner of Wakefield purchased the mortgage.

photo: Albert Jackson
Winter at Paradise Row

20

Later George Bustard Greaves, son of the unlucky Bank investor, acquired the house, while John Turner took charge at Hartshead House.

After the collapse Thomas Broadbent spent some time in Morocco before returning to Sheffield where he teamed up again with his brother Joseph – ducking and weaving in a factoring business before moving to Sandal, Wakefield where both brothers died within a month of each other in 1813. Thomas was then aged 63.

After the death in 1794 of John Turner, Hartshead House passed to his niece and into the Binney family of wealthy industrialists.

They erected furnaces on the land behind the house to pursue their steel making interests; they could be seen up to 1825 when the House became offices for the legal profession, initially by a solicitor named Copeland.

The House is now a Barrister's Chambers and known as Bank House Chambers.

photo: Albert Jackson

Bank House

photo: Albert Jackson
old Bank entrance

What was the old entrance to the Bank can still be seen under the arch of the building at   Hartshead, the door had now become a window.

Chapter Three

Plaques in the Square

Visitors to the Square will be intrigued to discover three plaques attached to the walls outside numbers 10, 24 and 3.
These are accredited to celebrities of their day, who had visited or utilised premises in the Square.

David Daniel Davis: arrived in the Square in 1803. He was born 15th June 1777, at Llandyfaslog, Carmarthenshire, as David Davies, the son of farmer Daniel Davies and mother Mary.

He was educated at Queen Elizabeth Grammar School, Carmarthen and the non-conformist Northampton Academy before taking his M.A. degree at Glasgow University. He qualified as a Non-Conformist Minister and as a Doctor of Medicine, specialising in mental illness.

Photo: Albert Jackson
Plaque outside Number 12

After leaving Glasgow, he practiced as a doctor in Mansfield while also holding a ministry at nearby Sutton in Ashfield.

Moving to Sheffield he took a position at the Sheffield Infirmary and was to change his name to David Daniel Davis in 1806, as he believed that it would make him stand alone rather than confuse him with others in the medical profession.

He married Catherine Hall at the Parish Church and they had their first child, a son, Henry Hall Davis on 20th April 1807, however he was to die from injuries caused at his birth by the delivery instruments.

This loss to them changed his career to devote his life to improving midwifery. He was elected in 1816 to physician-accocheur to the Northern Dispensary,

A second son, John Hall Davis was born in 1811, he was to follow his father and enjoy a distinguished career in medicine.

As he prospered, he moved away from the Square and was elected a Fellow of the Royal College of Physicians in Edinburgh and obtaining a licentiate with the Royal College in London in 1813.

In 1817 Princess Charlotte and her infant both died in the birth and lost the nation two generations of heir to the throne.

The following year the Duke of Kent married the German Princess of Saxe-Cobern and in the autumn came the announcement that the Duchess was expecting her first child and Dr David Daniel Davis would be responsible for the confinement.

He will be remembered for his role in delivering this child, who was later to become one of the greatest monarchs of this Country, Queen Victoria and also for his advancement of midwifery instruments.

photo: Albert Jackson

Illustration: Dennis Dalby

Retiring at 51 years of age in 1828 and died 13 years later after many years of poor health.

The medical profession in the Square were also to cause controversy when allegations were made against a Doctor.

Dr William Craig Ryves, L.R.C.P., L.R.C.S., L.M., was visited by Chief Inspector Moody and Detective Inspector Ibbotson of the Sheffield Constabulary, on Sunday 24th July 1898, arrested and taken to the Central Police Station.

He was later taken to visit 30-year-old Jane Mulhearn, at her home in Andrew Street, The Wicker, and confirmed to the Deputy Magistrates Clerk who had also attended, that she had undergone an operation performed by him.

Her deposition alleged that Dr Ryves had at her request performed an illegal abortion on her. The operation had not been satisfactory, and Mrs Mulhearn was in a critical condition.

Forty-one year old Dr Ryves appeared before the Magistrate and was remanded in custody for a week until bail could be arranged for him; his sureties were three of his friends.

At the hearing that followed the defence alleged that the woman had fallen down the stairs and had been drinking Gin before her miscarriage and that these were the true causes of it.

After careful deliberation with the Clerk of the Court, the Magistrate discharged the defendant; he stated that insufficient evidence of his guilt had been given by the prosecution.

Dr Ryves was to continue practising medicine from the Square until his retirement in 1920.

Sir Francis Legatt Chantry: was born in 1781, at Norton, then in the county of Derby. His father Francis, was a carpenter.

He was taught drawing by John Raphael Smith a noted engraver and he was to become both a famous painter and sculptor later in life.

Setting up a studio at number 24, in the Square he advertised in the 'Sheffield Iris' on April 22, 1802, that he would take sittings for portraits to be completed in crayons at his studio at 24, Paradise Square.

Photo: Albert Jackson
The Chantry plaque outside number 24

His advertisement continued… *"and trusts in being happy to produce good and satisfactory likenesses, and no exertion shall be wanted on his part, to render his humble efforts deserving some small share of public patronage".*

The cost of a miniature was between 2 and 3 guineas (£2.10 - £3.15) and his reputation was enhanced by work here and he counted several local dignitaries amongst his sitters.

He was to aspire to greater things and moved to London where after attending the Royal Academy was able to attract many more patrons and also branch into plaster casts and his favourite medium sculpture.

His statues and busts became much sought after and his subjects included several Royal pieces and many others of nobles and the rich and famous.

He did not forget his roots and maintained a home in Sheffield. He continued painting locally, not only portraits but also a series of drawings of the Rivelin valley.

Illustration: Dennis Dalby

He died on November 25th 1841, and such was his stature that it was suggested that he should be buried in Westminster Abbey, however his will was to be buried at Norton where he had reserved his burial plot, his wish was fulfilled and his tomb is in Norton Churchyard.

John Wesley: the founder of the Methodist Church and his younger brother Charles Wesley, were regular visitors to Sheffield. The plaque outside number 3, in the Square quotes the statement made by John Wesley... "I preached in Paradise Square in Sheffield to the largest congregation I ever saw on a weekday"

photo Albert Jackson
Plaque to John Wesley outside number 3

The waters were not always calm in those early days of Methodism for the two brothers from Epworth, near Doncaster.

John Wesley was born on 17th June 1703 and Charles on 18th December 1707.

The split from the established Church was not taken lightly and it spurred gangs to disrupt services and destroy buildings and property.

It was 1742 when John Wesley first visited Sheffield and met John Bennett at his small Meeting House in Cheney Square.

The following year he returned with his brother Charles and they were pelted with stones and filth. They escaped to Mr Bennett's home but the Meeting House was destroyed and demolished by the mob.

The next three Meeting Houses that were opened were likewise treated, yet the local authorities turned a blind eye to the events.

John Wesley appealed to the Church at York who decreed that the *Dissenters* were to be allowed to practice their faith peacefully and without interruption.

As a result of this, John Wesley and his followers were able to gain momentum and flourish enabling Wesley to take his beliefs overseas. He went to America where he took up the plight of slavery.

The plaque outside number 3 in the Square refers to his largest congregation on a weekday, St Swithin's Day, the 15th July 1779, when he addressed the crowd from the balcony of number 18

The following year, he was to preach inside Sheffield Cathedral, his preaching desk can be seen in the Chapter House below a stained glass window depicting his preaching in Paradise Square.

photo: Albert Jackson
The window at Sheffield Cathedral

His last visit to Sheffield was in June 1788, when he was aged 85.

When he stayed in Sheffield he bathed in the River Don at a point near where the Wicker Arches now cross it.

Illustration: Dennis Dalby

Links have been preserved with the Square. On the bi-centenary of the famous sermon in 1979, a pageant was held by the Methodist District Synod and the Square was packed with many followers in period costume.

The Rev. Joe Gibbon, a Methodist minister from Doncaster, rode on horseback into the Square to give a fiery oratory of a Wesley sermon from the same balcony.

In his work *'Early Future'*, local poet Geoffrey South wrote ...

> *Sloping historic*
> *This is Paradise Square*
> *where Wesley Preached*
> *on the same cobbles,*
> *under the same sky*
> *beneath chimneyed rain-gleam slate*
> *Shading the night sky*

© 2008 Geoffrey South

Chapter Four

House of Help

A reflection on the community can be judged on its ability to provide for the worse off and underprivileged. In this respect Sheffield has always had a positive response.

The House of Help for Friendless Girls and Young Women was the adopted title in 1890 of the Charity set up with Arthur

Davy as Treasurer, and Mrs Phoebe Flather as a very active Hon. Secretary in Fawcett Road, moving to Glossop Road, before making its home at Number 1, Paradise Square in 1885.

It had originally been named The Preventive and Rescue Society / House of Help and Mission Registry however The House of Help for Friendless Girls and Young Women was a more than accurate description of its aims and activities.

Known, it seems throughout the North of England, waifs and strays were left at the Railway Station or given a single ticket to Sheffield with instructions to report to the Station Master on their arrival, where they would be fed.

Imagine the sight of a poor young child, orphaned by her own family, confronted by the slow opening of the solid black front door of Number 1 Paradise Square, having been brought there for safety by a burly Police Constable.

Accommodation was of course also provided by the Workhouse at Fir Vale, however the House of Help provided a strict yet kind environment with vocational training, its volunteers and subscribers also willing to later take them into their homes as domestic servants.

It was not just the innocent that arrived at the door of Number 1. In Sheffield at the end of the 19th Century poverty and drunkenness led to crime and many girls were neglected and ran wild with little chance or desire to find work and better themselves.

The Magistrates often had their hearts touched by the girls before them and recommended a last chance for them at the House of Help, where they would, after being fed, bathed and de-loused, were given a clean bed and Tender Loving Care.

Next they would be fitted with new clothing and boots, the cost of which they would be expected to re-pay from any wages earned later.

On the occasion of a young "worldly wise" girl being referred; a harsh talking too would be administered to her before being admitted to ensure that she did not relate her experiences to the other girls.

As in most institutions, There were rules laid down for inmates…

GIRLS ELIGIBLE FOR ADMISSION

Young women who have fallen from virtue, and desire to redeem their character.

Young girls who have lost one or both parents, or who have parents living, should those parents be of loose character.

Girls of good character, who are not able to go to situations from want of clothing, are provided with outfits, which are afterwards paid for by arrangement between the Mistress and the Committee when situations have been procured for them.

Girls coming into town by train or otherwise, needing temporary lodgings are received at night.

Help is given to friendless girls who have recovered from illness in Hospitals, and have been compelled to pawn their clothing.

The time for remaining in the Preventative Branch of the House of Help is determined by the age, circumstances and requirements of each case.

Young persons are eligible, who have been placed in service from other institutions,

whose rules do not allow of their being re-admitted.

No girl of woman being intoxicated or uproarious in conduct can be admitted at any time to the Institution.

The Hon. Secretaries shall have discretional power to suspend any of these rules in urgent cases, which must afterwards be reported to the next Committee Meeting.

There were always more girls requiring help than the facilities available and this was a grave worry to the Trustees who realised that they must look out for larger premises.

Their prayers were answered in 1908 when the former 'Q' in the Corner / Shrewsbury Hotel at Number 17, became vacant after a fearful fire that had destroyed the entire *pub.*

A beneficiary came forward, he paid for the conversion and renovation of the building, leaving the House with just £80 to find to cover the removal.

They had raised £168. 5s. 6d. in advance of their advertising fundraising two day 'Sale of Work'.

On the first day of the sale, Lady Mary Howard, wife of the Duke of Norfolk, travelled from London to Sheffield for the opening. The second day was opened by the Lady Mayoress.

The 'two day sale' realised another £200 and the move went ahead without problem, however the increase in the size of the operation rocked the new House as rowdies took advantage of the situation for a time, until new staff could be recruited and trained.

Christmas was one of the highlights at the House, Old Girls were invited to visit and join in the festivities. Girls who had been in the House a full year received their own Bible, while girls who had been there for two years earned a reward of 5s. 0d. (25p).

There were also Benefactors who also made regular gifts to the House, on lady donated three gifts to each girl at Christmas and these were stored in a Bran-Tub prior to distribution. Another benefactor sent tea and rice every month for twenty-five years.

Number 17 was as successful as Number 1 had been, but times and the needs of the girls changed over the years and the House was able to keep pace with these changes. They could not unfortunately predict that their stay in the Square was coming to an end.

It was on the night of December 12/13th 1940 – the first night of the Sheffield Blitz, when Number 17 was the target for a direct hit by a German bomber, and was completely destroyed.

Seven girls and two staff had taken shelter in the cellars beneath the building and emerged the following morning shaken but otherwise unharmed and were able to eat a hearty breakfast before being taken to another home.

A survey revealed that there was no chance that the building could be restored during wartime and the search then began to find alternative accommodation.

It took just a year to find new premises that were suitable to their needs and to equip it to their requirements and on New Years Day 1942 the House of Help again opened its doors, this time on Glossop Road.

It was only in 2005, that the 'House' have been able to *pass the baton'* over to organisations that are better suited the modern day problems.

photo: Albert Jackson

Number 1 at night

Chapter Five

Entertainment

Throughout time the Square has provided leisure and entertainment for its visitors. Pubs and beer houses have always been plentiful and there have been four pubs around its cobbles and many others within its hinterland.

Of these 'The Q in the Corner' at number 17 is the most noted, its fame almost entirely due to the *Blind Fiddlers* who were amongst its customers.

The story had been told many times, that the Landlord of the 'Q', Sam Goodlad, was by his own description; *a man of the times,* travelling to London to visit the Music Halls and knowing all the latest *'Hits'.*

He would play these tunes to his customers and challenge all to be familiar with them. A prize of a leg of mutton was theirs if they were successful and could play them.

Maybe he should have learned his lesson, but often one of the *'Fiddlers'* would play the tune and claim the prize.

To achieve their scam, one of their number would squat down unseen while Sam played his latest hit, then *sneak* unseen outside, re-appearing in a blaze of activity, he would then play his tune to the onlookers. Sam could never understand how he had been bamboozled, but always honoured his debt.

The Fiddlers consisted of groups of musicians that spanned two generations, starting late in the eighteenth century and continuing to the middle of the next. Blind Stephen was the best known of them and was accompanied by George Smith and John Gibbons.

They had a circuit of public houses where they played, and these had to be fiercely protected from intruders. They were competent musicians and also played at a Concert by six prominent Blind Musicians arranged by the Sheffield Blind institute at the Assembly Rooms on Norfolk Street on May 3rd 1810.

Illustration: Dennis Dalby

On one dark and smoggy night Blind Stephen asked for a lantern before leaving, explaining that it was not for him to be see, but to be seen as he didn't want to risk somebody damaging his violin by bumping into him.

The 'Q' was to later become the Shrewsbury Hotel, when after a refit it became an American Theme Bar.

At number 11, the sign over the door proclaimed it to be known as the "Crown", while across the Square number 22 the "The Clown and Monkey" / "Yorkshire Clown" had a less savoury reputation.

"The Clown and Monkey" was the venue for the rat fighting pit, where in the cellar dogs were released into the rat pit, bets were placed on the dog that would kill the most rats.

The rats were bred on the premises or bought for 1s (5p) a dozen, but often escaped their cages to infest the rest of the Square.

It must have been one of the Town's most unruly areas with the drunkenness and outlandish behaviour. On more than one occasion the Town's Magistrates were presented with landlord William Cliffe on charges of running a disorderly beer house and was fined 50s. (£2.50p) with 8s.0d (20p) costs on this occasion.

A neighbour, surgeon Mr Booth, had made a complaint that Cliffe was running a house that was " the resort of thieves, dog fighters and the lowest possible company". After an afternoons fun rat fighting, an assembly totalling more that 150 had surged into the Square fighting and stumbling about until a pitched battle erupted amongst the market stalls during Market Day.

Today, the Square is again host to a Bar / Restaurant - "The Wig and Pen" on Campo Lane, extended into the Square in 2008, providing an amiable ambiance to the cobbles with outdoor benches and tables.

The extension was not without its objectors, principally the English Heritage were keen to preserve the tranquility of the Square and several tenants were also pessimistic about the affair.

In hindsight, all the objections have been satisfied and the cobbles again ring with the laughter of people enjoying themselves on the outdoor tables and benches provided.

This could be the beginning of a new era in the Square where events could be held and the public attracted back.

Nearby is the Three Tuns pub on Silver Street Head The present pub built in 1843, is on the site of an earlier Three Tuns, and is a busy traditional pub popular with local bank workers.

It is said to be haunted, yet another building where strange feelings have been experienced over the years although no *ghost* has been seen, there have been temperature changes and mysterious happenings.

The cellars have bricked up archways, indicating that tunnels have existed from there to places unknown.

From the reproduced advertisement, which appeared in The Sheffield & Rotherham Independent on April 8th, 1843, it can be seen that a brewery existed on the premises, much in the same style as the 'modern' *micro-breweries* that exist today.

To LICENSED VICTUALLERS.

TO BE LET, with Immediate Possession, the NEW INN, lately Erected on the Site of the OLD THREE TUNS PUBLIC-HOUSE, situate at the Junction of Silver street head and Lee croft, containing a Spacious BREWERY, Extensive DEEP CELLARING, KITCHEN, PARLOUR, BAR, and DRAM-SHOP; an Excellent CLUB-ROOM, 42 feet long; and FIVE LODGING ROOMS.

This House is situate in one of the greatest Thoroughfares in Sheffield, and is admirably adapted for carrying on an extensive Business, possessing also the rare advantage of a Private Brewery.

Application to be made to Mr. WILLIAM RAGG, Nursery, Sheffield.

courtesy of Sheffield Local History Library.
Newspaper advertisement from 1843

42

At the bottom of the Hill on Bank Street the *Three Cranes* provides food and drink, as they have done for most of the existence of the Square.

Should you travel down Paradise Street (formerly Workhouse Lane), then continue into Russell Street; the Kelham Island Tavern (formerly the White Hart) was constructed by a builder who lived in the Square.

Quite often the Author and Illustrator can be found there. The *"Kelham Island Tavern"* has been voted best Sheffield Pub and also won the award of Best Beer Garden in the Sheffield in Bloom competitions both over several consecutive years.

The Square contains remnants from the ruins of Sheffield Castle, which was demolished after the Civil War. Stone, timber and doors were salvaged and put to good use both in the Square and also in surrounding streets.

It is now, when demolition and rebuilding of the City Centre is prolific, that this part of Sheffield's history is reappearing.

The 'Q in the Corner', at Number 17, received a makeover when it became an American Theme Bar – The Shrewsbury Hotel. The manager, George E. Jacobs lived on the premises along with his unmarried sister and three members of staff.

He had completely changed the décor and mood of the establishment, having spent over £200 in re-decoration.

The *Dram Shop* was treated in a novel manner with virgin cork being employed in the ornamentation of the room, which was furnished with an aviary and a well stocked aquarium.

A wide amount of rustic brackets were hanging with choice flowers and plants. Working models were also displayed around the premises, along with many other interesting objects.

Plate glass and ornamental bar fittings, mirrors and lavish furniture adorned the smoke-room and the other areas.

It had a Skittle Alley, the forerunner of the Bowling Alley and a sign adorned the outside telling all of its "American Bowling".

The Shrewsbury Hotel became home to the No. 1 "Shrewsbury Lodge" of The Order of Buffaloes.

The Hotel came to a sad ending when in the early hours of Friday October 27th 1882, a fire was spotted by a passer by at twenty past two in the morning and he alerted Police Constable James Walsh before running to the Fire office where Superintendent Pound mobilised his fire crew.

The fire brigade arrived on the scene promptly to discover the fire raging through the premises. P.C. Walsh had managed to awaken the inhabitants, who had been safely evacuated.

Casualties were limited to the family cat and dog together with the birds and fish, although the pub was completely destroyed and left boarded up for several years.

Punishment for being drunk or being found drinking on a Sunday or when a Church service was in progress was a visit to the stocks. These had been outside the Cathedral but were moved into the Square. They were last used in about 1830.

At the same time the remains of the Old Irish Cross also took its place in the Square, it was removed to become a major exhibit in the National History Museum in London, while a cast taken from it was taken to Weston Park Museum, Sheffield.

It was placed on the plinth that originally had held a pump and was later to be replaced by the *famous gas lamp.*

The Gas lamp was a favourite vantage point for hecklers at the meetings conducted from the balcony of Number 18.

Tuesday was the day that the Earthenware Market was held in the Square, because of this the Square became known colloquially as the *Pot Square* during this period.

Originally held outside the Cathedral, the market was moved into the Square after Dam Hall, Constable and Beadle, who lived in the Square and had a crockery shop, suggested it to John White, the Markets Clerk.

The Square at this time had transformed with the surrounding Crofts into having many traders and warehouses on the ground floor properties, many specialising in pots and crockery.

With the market came the euphoria of stallholders plying their trades, the tossing of plates and barter were commonplace.

Well documented is the merchandise sold in the market, although there were times when it was not directly in keeping with pots, although there was a common denominator that linked the two – Wives !

Two wives were reputedly sold in the Pot Market, the first was the wife of John Lees, a steel-burner who sold his wife to Samuel Hall for just 6d (2½p), she was taken to the Market with a horses halter around her neck.

The price had risen for the second sale, this time the price was five shillings (25p), a watch and a gold chain. The Lady was said to have been pleased with the transaction.

The Town Crier was a regular attendant at the opening of the market in the Square and also appeared in the streets around it.

Illustration: Dennis Dalby

45

As time progresses it is hoped that further festivities will be permitted in the Square which not only has to comply with the wishes of the Shrewsbury Hospital and Town Trustees Trusts, but falls within the Sheffield Council bye-laws and English Heritage protection.

In recent times 'Street Theatre' has been performed in the Square and plans are being discussed to allow these to develop. In addition to the Carol Service, it is hoped that a large outdoor ChristmasTree will be erected along with an annual Christmas Market.

Photograph: Albert Jackson
Street Theatre in the Square with the Maze Players

Chapter Six

Education

At the time when Sheffield offered its children very little in the way of education, other than the Sunday Schools provided by the Church, the Square excelled by providing private academies to educate those children whose parents had the ability to pay.

On the first floor of number 18 Paradise Square, at the top of the stone staircase was the Johannes Chapel room. Originally the Masonic Lodge, when they moved to the Wicker, the Chapel used the room for both earth and heavenly instruction.

The Chapel moved to a more permanent location and after being used as a dancing school the premises were advertised as an ideal location as a meeting room.

Edward Hebblethwaite, a recently qualified teacher from the Lancastarian School, was one day walking through the town centre and into the Square, where he saw that the upper floor of Number 18 was empty and he realised that he could fulfil his dream by opening his own academy school there.

The Hebblethwaite Academy School for Boys opening in 1811 and most of its pupils came away with a magnificent grounding for their futures in Commerce and Industry or to further their academic careers.

There was at least one exception to the success story; Charles Edward Peace, born May 14th 1832, the son of a one legged Lion Tamer (failed!).

He was to become the infamous Charlie Peace, a master criminal and amorous murderer.*

*A resume of his treacherous Sheffield murder is highlighted in the Appendix.

Illustration by Dennis Dalby

Edward Hebblethwaite remained at his Academy until he retired in 1865.

Arthur Newell bought the Academy from Hebblethwaite and continued its activities by…

> a) extending into number 20,
> b) by the admission of girls and

c) changing the name to The Middle Class School for boys and girls.

A recent refurbishment of number 20 exposed many sets of initials carved into the window ledges. Tops of the desks and tables were also found as storage surfaces in the cellar.

Changing its leadership for James Longstaffe to become Headmaster, its days were becoming numbered as both the state and private education had advances in later years and the War had limited resources. The school finally closed its doors in 1937.

The north-west corner of the Square had an attraction for the scholar, the Jewish fraternity, many of whom had reached Sheffield as migrants from eastern Europe, settled in the Croft areas around the Square.

The Shul situated in North Church Street, had been built in 1872 and Hebrew lessons were given there, another at West Bar Green, had a room where lessons were also given. In 1902 the Talmud Torah opened new schoolrooms with four classes above a butchers shop at West Bar.

In 1904 the vacant post of Headmaster was filled by Saul Finklestone of Leeds. He took up his post, bringing with him his wife and four children, and was to remain in the post as a successful Headmaster for the next thirty-one years.

On September 11th the same year, news of new premises in Paradise Square were announced. It was also stated that girls would also be taught at the new school.

The grand opening of the school was on February 20th 1905. 600 people filled the Square where the children sang.

The school finally outgrew the Square in 1924, when a move was made to new larger premises in Brunswick Street.

Saul Finklestine retired in 1935, and died in August of the same year.

photo courtesy of David Grunwerg / E.D. Saylis

Number 22 -Sheffield Hebrew School – 1910
Coronation celebrations of George V and Queen Mary
S.H. Finklestine Headmaster, (Top Hat) R. Resse, L. Abrahams
and M. Goldblum

There were female seminaries operated over the years at numbers 5, 7 & 9, teaching young ladies the etiquette of life and preening them for marriage.

The House of Help which began its work in the Square at number 1 in 1885, moving to number 17 in 1908, catered for the less fortunate young females and instructed them in their basic educational needs.

In East Parade was the Boy's Charity School later to be known as the Blue Coat School. Established in 1706 it provided a basic education, meals and clothing for poor boys.

They boys were often *'lent out'* by the masters as cheap labour, they would then spend their days gambling and cavorting.

The original building was replaced in 1825, then it had a playground built on its roof, later it was to move to a larger site with a playing field on Psalter Lane.

photo: Albert Jackson
Poor Girls School – St James' Row

The original building was replaced in 1825, then it had a playground built on its roof, later it was to move to a larger site with a playing field on Psalter Lane.

This then became the College of Art, but it closed in 2008 for re-development as houses and apartments. The School building retained and tastefully adapted as apartments.

On the other side of the then Parish Church, in St James' Row, was the Girl's Charity School erected in 1786. The original building, with its plaque can be seen on the façade above the upper floor. The original school was to move to Mount Pleasant in 1825.

Illustration: Dennis Dalby
Irish Cross

Moved into the Square, the stump of the Cross was erected on its steps ion the centre. When gas first arrived, the lamp was fitted to the top.

Chapter Seven

Public Meetings – Prayer and Punches

Number Eighteen Paradise Square had its first floor rooms accessible from a stone staircase protruding eighteen feet (5.75m) into the Square. At the top of this the balcony provided the ideal rostrum for Public Meetings.

Illustration: Dennis Dalby

John Wesley and his brother Charles were regular visitors to Sheffield and on many occasions used the Square to preach to their followers. Their meetings also attracted agitators and extremists from the Established Church, they objected to the Methodism of Wesley and were also responsible for the burning down and destruction of his meeting rooms.

The balcony provided the ideal forum, the Square sloped down and all of the spectators were able to have a clear view of the speaker.

An important tool for those whose objectives at the meeting were disruption, was heckling. The Square had a vantage point for the dedicated heckler, the gaslamp in the centre of the Square. Straddled across this, the heckler stood out from the crowd and was virtually on eye level with the speaker. If the heckler earned the backing of the crowd, the speaker was like a fox surrounded by the pack of hounds.

courtesy of Sheffield Local History Library
Political Meeting in the Square c. 1890

Such was the case that the Chartists, began to hold anti government meetings, one of the well known of their movement was Samuel Holberry.

Winter of 1837 saw the Sheffield Rivers frozen, with the ice so thick that skaters were served with sheep that had been roasted on the ice.

It was also the formation of the Sheffield Working Men's Association – their aim was to win the vote for the workingman. Public meetings were their tools for transmitting their opinions to parliament – Paradise Square was their chosen venue.

Their intention was to achieve their aims by peaceful means and attracted speakers with a like objective.

Ebenezer Elliott, the poet known as the *Corn Rhymer,* was happy to lend his name to the cause and also wrote several poems describing the hardship and suffering of the poor. He also made several passionate speeches from the balcony in the Square, but he became disillusioned by the workings of the movement and resigned from it.

There was an element that did not have the patience or desire to protest '*by the book'*. They agitated for violence and began to have a bigger and bigger following around Sheffield.

On several occasions disruption was serious enough for the militia to be called and the crowds disbursed.

Meetings were then held above Sheffield at Skye Edge, silent protests were held in the Parish Church, author Charles Dickens visited Sheffield to observe the happenings and used some of his findings in *'Oliver Twist'.*

Despite a ban on public meetings by the Magistrates, on September 12th 1839, troops were called to a meeting being held in the Square. When they arrived, the gas lamps illuminating the Square had been extinguished and the crowd, said to number over 2,000 had set an ambush and attacked the Dragoons with sticks, stones and other weapons, the running battle spread to the churchyard and Arundle Street resulting in 36 arrests.

Illustration: Dennis Dalby

Rumours were rife that the Chartists were amassing weapons in preparation of an uprising and the Magistrates instigated an intelligence network to spy on the activists.

Unrest became more common and buildings and property were looted and property including weapons stolen.

The escalation of the violence did not meet with the ideals of all the remaining members, however Holberry ruled them with a rod of steel and continually threatened them with a pistol, that he would 'blow their brains out' if they did not follow him.

The Magistrates 'intelligence' paid off when a report of a plot was given them. It was for that very night and the Town Hall and Tontine Hotel were amongst the targets to be captured and held, while other groups were to make similar attacks in Nottingham and Dewsbury.

Holberry and the other leaders were quickly rounded up and charged with conspiracy to riot, and taken to York for trial at the Assizes. Weapons comprising guns with ammunition, knives, pikes, bombs, hand grenades and bayonets were also seized.

Holberry was found guilty and sentenced to four years in gaol at the Northallerton House of Correction, where he was tortured. He developed consumption and was transferred to York Castle, where he died on 21st June 1842 and buried in the General Cemetery. At least 50,000 people followed the funeral cortege from Attercliffe to attend his burial at the General Cemetery.

A fountain was dedicated to his memory and after the building work near the Town Hall, it was replavled by a plaque of Welsh Slate and 'The Holbery Cascades" in the Peace Gardens.

After several years of keeping their heads low, the Chartists grew popular again, but at a meeting of the activist Fergus O'Connor in 1844, only 150 people witnessed it. They peeked and troughed after this, supporting almost every 'good cause'.

Paradise Square was never to experience the trauma of such meetings again.

Politicians were the other users of the 'balcony', those who had been elected and those that wished they could be. Many debates were also conducted.

The removal of the staircase to be replaced by an internal stairway was as much to conclude the use of the Square for public meetings as to improve the properties amenities.

Chapter Eight

Solicitors

Many of the original occupants of the five houses, known then as Paradise Row, later forming the East side of the Square, were from the legal profession.

As times changed and the Square and its surroundings became less attractive to the wealthy classes; market traders, publicans and their followers became the majority, yet, not taking over the Square exclusively.

Then, the legal men returned in might, transforming the Square into what exists today.

Early incomers were the Wheat dynasty; today, the family have spread to the four corners of the globe. Family reunions gather them back to examine their origins and provide in itself something spectacular.

Dating back to the early eighteenth century, James Wheat first appeared in the Square, taking a lease on three houses on the south side in 1776.

They then moved into Paradise Row and were to remain there until the death of J.B. Wheat in 1936.

James Wheat also purchased Norwood Hall, in 1775, a fine old house, dating back to the sixteenth century, with a Queen Ann core.

During the civil unrest in 1791, his friend and Magistrate; Rev. James Wilkinson of Broom Hall, was besieged by a riotous mob and the Hall ransacked.

Hearing that they were also targeting him, James Wheat moved his family to safety and employed a guard. Damage to his property was thus confined to the burning down of a barn.

The Hall remained in the family until the death of John James Wheat in 1915, when the estate was split up.

The house later became the home of Sheffield's first Bishop; Dr Leonard Hedley Burrows, and was renamed *'Bishopsholme'*.

J. B. Wheat was conceived late in his father's life and as a result J. B. grew up to be a frail and thin man. He was to inherit the nickname 'Shredded Wheat'.

James Wheat was a prominent lawyer of the period and had among his many successes the prosecution of Frank Fearn for the murder of watchmaker Nathan Andrews. After the trial Fearn was hanged and his body gibbeted on Loxley Edge on March 27th 1782.

Joseph Mather, the Sheffield songwriter, penned a song to the events, a verse explains...

> *At Kirk Edge I shot and stabbed him,*
> *Cut his throat and bruis'd his pate*
> *Of his watch and money robbed him*
> *Causes my unhappy fate.*

The firm of Bramley and Coombe evolved from solicitors practising in the Square; the Bramley arm was founded in 1817 by Joseph Haywood who moved into the Square in 1821, Edward Bramley was articled and admitted as a solicitor in 1828. After a period practicing on his own account he became a partner in 1841.

There were several comings and goings over the years until on 1st January 1920, Edward Bramley joined forces with Charles Stanley Coombe.

They carried on their business from number 6, since 1821, and had since the Incorporation of Sheffield in 1843, acted on behalf of the Corporation from their offices.

60

Edward Bramley was the first Town Clerk, and was succeeded by Herbert Bramley in October 1895, a position he maintained until his death in 1897.

The Coombe pedigree was founded in 1788 by John Brookfield in 1788, he was succeeded by Charles Brookfield and joined by Thomas Gould and subsequently by John Newbould, when the firm became Newbould & Gould.

Evaluation admitted John Newton Coombe as a partner and after his death, Charles Stanley Coombe, his son. He was to merge with Edward Bramley.

The premises were sold by Mr Coombe for £1,500 to Mr Bramley.

They had been at number 4, since 1803 and after the merger the business of Bramley and Coombe was conducted from number 6, with an additional two rooms in # 4.

Mr Heywood and his successors rented number 6, at a cost of £35 per annum, which rose to £50 per annum, when in 1891 it was bought by Herbert Bramley for £1,000.

When it was purchased the price included a garden with a Brewhouse, Laundry and Stable. A strongroom was built on the site of the Stable and Laundry and the office extended.

The Company of Bramley & Coombe continued until 1950 when it then merged with Branson's then into Keeble Hawson and now has its offices in adjacent St James' Row.

The office of 'Lord Clerk' to the Sheffield Town Trust then passed from Richard Bramley to the present holder George Connell, a partner with Keeble Hawson.

Commissioned into the Hallamshire Battalion of the York & Lancaster Regiment in 1910, Douglas Stephenson Branson joined the Company after returning from War service in 1919.

He took a law 'crammer' and after only six months intensive course he took his law examination, passing with considerable distinction in February 1920, and was admitted as a solicitor in June 1920, joining the Company.

His military career was to make him the Hallamshires' most renowned and remarkable soldier. At the age of 23, in 1917, he was to command the Battalion, gaining 3 D.S.O's in 10 months having previously been awarded the Military Cross.

In addition to his professional activities he was to become Hon. Colonel Sir Douglas Branson K.B.E., C.B., D.S.O., T.D., D.L. after devoting his loyalty to the Hallamshires' through the Territorial Army.

The premises once known to its builder as 'Broadbent's Buildings', then Paradise Row, now numbers 4 – 12 Paradise Square, are occupied by solicitors Graysons.

At the time of the merger in 1920, three of the five buildings in the row had been occupied by solicitors for over a century.

Today of the twenty-six properties comprising the four faces of the Square, no less than eleven are occupied by solicitors and another two by Barristers Chambers.

Chapter Nine

Carol Service

A tradition was started over twenty years ago by the legal profession of the Square after Radio Sheffield ended their annual torchlight carol service from the Square.

courtesy and © 2008 Terry Gorman
'Paradise Square' by Terry Gorman

Christmas has always been a time for joy and celebration in the Square. Whatever their trade or profession the inhabitants held the festival season high in their priorities.

The local radio station – Radio Sheffield – for many years broadcast their Annual Christmas Carol Concert from the Square. The Salvation Army providing its Band for the occasion.

Each year in the run up to Christmas, the Square used to be closed off and the vehicles moved from their reserved parking places.

A large stage was speedily erected on the cobbles of the Square in preparation for the evening when they broadcast took over their airwaves.

Although an annual event, protocol decreed that it was necessary for permission to use the Square be obtained from Sheffield Town Trust.

The choristers, dressed in scarves and bobble hats, held long candles while they filled the Square with their enthusiastic rendering of their carols to their musical accompaniment.

The inclement weather was a major contributor to the decision to move the concerts to indoor venues, the final concert was held on Sunday December 19th 1993.

The void left was quickly filled when Adam Pemberton, then a partner with solicitor's Watson Esam, as well as a hobby saxophonist, amassed fellow legal contemporaries from nearby offices, along with family and friends to provide a substitute event.

The concerts were performed by his band of musicians from the balcony of the offices of Watson Esam, at number 18, the point from where John Wesley had preached to the crowds some two - hundred years earlier.

The musicians also provided minced pies, fruit juice and mulled wine to the public and staff from the offices around, who came to sing along with them.

The concert is held at lunchtime on the last working day before the Christmas break. Each year a charity is nominated to receive the donations from a collection which is made.

As the years go by, the musicians have grown in number to the point where they now play from the pavement amongst the songsters.

Illustration: Dennis Dalby

The Square should in future years have an outdoor Christmas Tree to further enhance the Festive spirit.

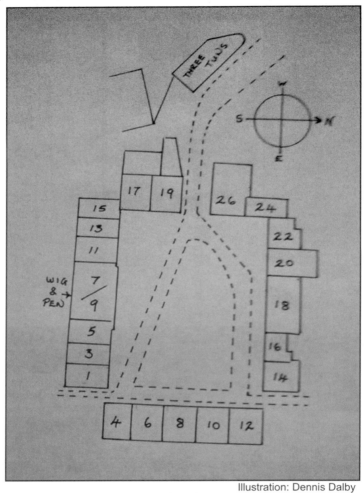

Illustration: Dennis Dalby

Plan of the Square

Chapter Ten

Looking through the Windows

Each building in the Square is unique, both in its design, use, and of the characters that have walked over their thresholds. A selection of these is highlighted along with a resume of some of the tenants over the last one and a half centuries.

photo: Albert Jackson
South face of Square (1 – 15)
(view shows outside the Wig & Pen)

Number 1 – The building is best known as the original House of Help, it first opened its doors in 1885, to the poor and destitute women and girls who had found life's low. They moved to larger premises at number 17 in 1908.

When the Square was built, the leases of numbers 1 – 11 were awarded to James Wheat, however he was later to exchange these for 'Broadbent's building's' – the original name of numbers 4 – 12, where the family still hold them to-day.

Number 1 had been a *'beerhouse'* and what is now the side entrance had been The Clarence Hotel, the Highway Office and is currently a Letting Agent.

photo: Albert Jackson
Number 1

Directories:
1854 – George Marples - Solicitor
1883 – Richard Marshall – Dining rooms.
1905 – House of Help for Girls and Young Women.
1920 – George Harry Bray – Accountant
      Midland Films Ltd. – Film rentals
1973 – William Gregory & Co. – Estate Agents.
2008 – W. D. Flowers – Chartered accountants.

Number 3 – Outside here is the John Wesley plaque, identifying his preaching in the Square on St. Swithen's Day 1779. He had though, preached from the balcony at the top of the stone steps that were at number 18.

John Heiffor & Co., were users of stainless steel, their cutthroat razor was exported to all four corners of the globe. It is still much sought after as an antique / collectors piece and examples can often be found on computer sale rooms.

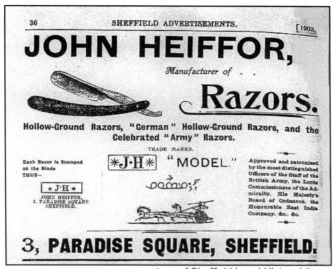

courtesy of Sheffield Local History Library
Heiffor Razors 1903

They produced an 'army' razor, approved by the Lords of the Admiralty, Board of Ordnance, The East India Company and many officers of the British Army thus ensuring its success.

Illustration: Dennis Dalby

They were to change the method of shaving by perfecting a *'modern'* Hollow-ground razor.

Established in 1798, the Heiffor family were in business for over a century,
the founder John Heiffor, is buried with his family in Christ Church Pitsmoor.

Directories:
1854 – William Bellamy – Sheriffs' Officer.
1883 – John Heiffor – Razor manufacturer.
1905 – John Heiffor – Razor manufacturer
1920 – John Heiffor – Razor manufacturer
1973 – Parkin, Bainbridge & Co. – Chartered accountants.
2008 – Hodgson & Oldfield – Accountants.

Number 5 - Along with numbers 7 & 9, they have all had the distinction over the years to operate as *Ladies Seminaries*. Many other trades and professions have also been here, When the *Pot Market* was held in the centre cobbles, many crockery, pot and china dealers also had premises in the Square, generally the ground floors had shop frontages having changed from housing to professional premises then later, in the middle of the Twentieth Century, they began to revert to the classic style that we have today.

photo: Albert Jackson
Nos. 5, 7 & 9 (Wig & Pen) and 11

70

Directories:
1854 – vacant
1883 – Samuel Parker
1905 – Brookes Bros. – Printers.
    Provident Free Home Assurance Co. Ltd.
1920 – Joseph Arthur Darwent – Accountant.
    Albert E. Brookes – Commission Agent.
    The Sheffield & District Confectioner's Assoc. – J. A. Darwent –Sec.
    Sheffield Tradesman's Plate Glass Guar. Soc. Ltd. - A Thorpe - Sec.
    Sheffield & District Master Baker's Assoc. – J. A. Darwent – Sec.
    Metal Dealers' and Waste Trades Assoc. - J. A. Darwent – Sec.
    Sheffield & District Whol. Product Exchange - J. A. Darwent – Sec.
1973 – John Sanderson & Son. – Estate Agents.
    Arthur Darwent & Co. – Certified accountant and auditor.
    Dewsbury & West Riding Building Society.
2008 – Narrow Estates Ltd – Estate management.

Number 7 – Now numbers 7 and 9 are the Wig & Pen, a restaurant and bar, which has extended from its original premises on Campo Lane into the Square providing it with a *Continental*, yet traditional air.

Over the years Surgeons, House Agents, a lodging house, pot and china dealers, have all traded from here however it is in recent times that the tenants of number 7 have been colourful.

D'arcy Staniland Dye (George to senior staff and family) was a quantity surveyor and extremely extravert, moving into the Square in the early 1950's.

Born in Sleaford in 1917, the name Staniland was his Grandmothers maiden name. He met his wife, a nurse at the Royal Hospital on West Street, while having an operation on his *lazy eye.* They later had three children who were all to carry on the 'Staniland Dye' name.

D'arcy maintained that number 7 was haunted and a female member of staff often complained of an 'atmosphere' – no explanation can be found, however, D'arcy also told of a Circus troupe who had lodged there, they returned every year at the end of the season – yet again no trace of them exists.

They purchased their T bags from a café lower down the hill, however when they required a 'brew' the junior was despatched to the café with the teapot containing teabags to be filled with boiling water – free of charge.

He was a Member of the Chartered Institute of Architects and was favoured by several large Sheffield clients including Ackroyd and Abbot, Weston Senior and the Sheffield Rolling Mills. The business continued until his retirement in 1977.

When they moved into, number 7, it was also occupied by a plumber – J. S. Blackburn & Co., they had the ground floor and a workshop in the backyard. The first floor housed Maurice Darwent, a Debt Collector and Private Investigator, he was a *'strange little man'* with an attractive wife, and she ran the office.

D'arcy made extensive alterations to the premises when he gained sole tenancy, installing a lithograph press in the vaulted cellars in order to print his own 'Bills of Quality'.

Estate Agents Patrick Crapper and Son, moved into the Square in 1984, having previously been in York Street and Fig Tree Lane. He remained in the Square until 2007, when he moved out of the Square after 23 years and into nearby St James House, to make way for the Wig & Pen extension.

Patrick was joined in the Square by Albert Jackson (no relation of the writer), who acted as a consultant to him. Previously, Albert (Bert) had been a senior partner at Eadon, Lockwood and Riddle, and was also a City Magistrate and a Director of Sheffield United Football Club.

Patrick and Bert formed a formidable team, know and respected not just in the Square, but also throughout the City.

Albert Jackson died in 2008.

Directories:
1854 – John Clayton – Auctioneer, valuer, house and estate agent
1883 – 7 & 9 Hugh Watson Harrison - Surgeon
1905 – 7 & 9 Hugh Watson Harrison - Surgeon
1920 – J. S. Blackburn & Co. – Plumbers.
1973 – D'arcy Dye & Associates – Quantity surveyors.
2008 – 7 & 9 – Wig and Pen – Restaurant and Bar

Number 9 – One of the earliest buildings to have been connected to an adjoining building, it has at one time been a home to The Central Radical Club, which later became the Reform Club with a fine Gothic style building built in 1885, and then rebuilt as offices behind its original façade in St James Row.

Directories:
1854 – William Hastings - Draper
1883 – 7 & 9 Hugh Watson Harrison - Surgeon
1905 – 7 & 9 Hugh Watson Harrison - Surgeon
1920 – Holmes, Widlake & Gibson – Chartered accountants.
    Scottish Provident Institution – William Holmes, District agent.
1973 – vacant
2008 – 7 & 9 – Wig and Pen – Restaurant and Bar

Number 11 – The 'Old Cock Tavern' – one of the four pubs to have been in the Square was here in the first half of the nineteenth century, it did not have a reputation like those of the 'Q' or the Clown.

By contrast, a Police Institute was opened in 1897, by Sir Charles Skelton. He had been Mayor in 1894 and was on the Police Committee. It was in 1894 that H.M. Queen Victoria bestowed the title "Lord Mayor" to its First Citizen.

Directories:
1854 – Old Cock Tavern – Edmund Inkersall
1883 – Joseph Pearson – Accountant etc.
    The Abbeydale Freehold Land Society
    Highfield Club Building Company Limited
    13th Patriotic Benefit Building Society
        Joseph Pearson – Secretary.
1905 – Police Institute – Richard Hopkins, caretaker.
1920 – Police Institute – Arthur Wilson, caretaker.
1973 – vacant
2008 – D. I. P. Consultants – Management consultants.

Number 13 – It was glass and chinaware that made its biggest impact at number 13. The Square became known as 'Pot Square' from early in the 1800's,continuing for most of the century.

Slum housing called 'The Crofts', which were replaced by tenements and office blocks, heavily populated the surrounding areas. The tenements in their turn became inadequate and have been redeveloped.

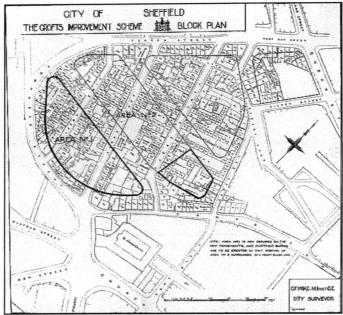

courtesy of Sheffield Local Study Library
The Crofts showing re-development plans.

The surroundings have in later years attracted quality apartment blocks and in keeping with the Square, become the place to have an address.

Directories:
1854 – Henry Whitford – Glassware & china warehouse
1883 – Robert Blackburn - Clerk
1905 – Walter Eagers & Son. – Rent bailiffs.
1920 – Peter Hanson.
1973 – 13 & 15 – Waite & Co. - Solicitors
2008 – 13, 15 & 17 - Hale Saunders – Chartered Surveyors.
         Marriot Gibbs, Rees Wallace – Chartered accountants,
         Auditors and Tax consultants.

Number 15 – Another building of mixed usage.

Directories:
1854 – Mr William Hatfield.

74

1883 – William Henry Parkin – Tailor.
1905 – vacant
1920 – Mrs Flora Gregson – Householder.
1973 – 13 & 15 – Waite & Co. - Solicitors
2008 – 13, 15 & 17 – Hale Saunders – Chartered Surveyors.
Marriot Gibbs, Rees Wallace – Chartered accountants, Auditors and Tax consultants.

Number 17 – The much renowned 'Q' in the Corner pub, became the Shrewsbury Hotel (an American themed pub) only to be burned down in the early hours of Friday October 27th, 1882.

photo: Albert Jackson
Nos. 17 & 19
formerly the 'Q' in the Corner and theHouse of Help

Rebuilt in 1908, for the House of Help, they occupied numbers 17 and 19 until the first night of the Sheffield Blitz in 1940, when it was destroyed yet again, this time by an enemy bomb.

Rebuilt, it has had a variety of tenants and has just had a fresh refurbishment when the heavily charred timbers of the Shrewsbury Hotel fire had to be removed and replaced.

Directories:
1854 – 'Q' in the Corner Inn – Edward Harrison
1883 – Shrewsbury Hotel – George Edward Jacobs.
1905 – vacant
1920 – 17&19 House of Help for Girls & Young Women–Miss L. Jones,Matron
1973 – Walter Bell & Co. – Accountants.
2008 – 13, 15 & 17 - Hale Saunders – Chartered Surveyors.
                     Marriot Gibbs, Rees Wallace – Chartered accountants,
                     Auditors and Tax consultants.

Number 19 – Although rebuilt after the Sheffield Blitz in December 1940, fittings such as the downpipe were rescued and show the original date of 1777. The property had been part of the House of Help, which after the bombing moved away.

photo: Albert Jackson
Head of Downpipe at No.19

Directories:
1854 – Mrs Ann Smith – Furniture broker.
1883 – George Fletcher – Machine and tool broker.
1905 – vacant
1920 – 17&19 House of Help for Girls & Young Women–Miss L. Jones,Matron
1973 – Moore, Fletcher, Fosdike & Sons. – Chartered accountants.
2008 – vacant

76

4 – 12 Paradise Row (Broadbent's Buildings)

These properties were built by Thomas Broadbent in 1735, and were the predecessors of the Square fronting Hick's Stile Field. The lease on these five houses was £5 (£1 each) per annum and now on their frequent visits to Sheffield, a member of the Wheat family will present their £5 Ground Rent to the Shrewsbury Trust Office.

The Row was built on a true North - South line, thus reference to the side of the Square is completely accurate.

photo courtesy of Keeble Hawson
Broadbent's Building 1963
(The Corsair & Kit car belong to Partners of Blackburn & Co. (Number 14)

Number 4.

Directories:
1854 – Thomas Gould - Solicitor
1883 – Newbould & Gould – Solicitors.
1905 – Gould & Coombe - Solicitor
1920 – Gould & Coombe - Solicitor
      Miss Winifred Tomlinson A.L.C.M. – Teacher of Piano.
1973 – 4 & 6 – Branson, Bramley & Co. – Solicitors, commissioners for oaths.
2008 – 4 to 12 – Graysons – Solicitors.

Number 6.

Directories:
1854 – Bramley & Gainsford – Solicitors
      Edward Bramley – Town Clerk
1883 – Herbert Bramley – Solicitor & Agent – *Economic Life Assurance Co.*
1905 – Bramley & Son – Solicitor

Edward Bramley – Solicitor
Fraser Herbert Bramley – Architect
Sheffield Crematorium Co. Ltd. – Edward Bramley, Hon. Sec.
1920 – Bramley & Son – Solicitors
Edward Bramley M.A. - Solicitor
1973 – 4 & 6 – Branson, Bramley & Co. – Solicitors, commissioned for oaths.
2008 – 4 to 12 – Graysons – Solicitors.

Number 8 .

Directories:
1854 – John James Wheat – Solicitor, Clerk to *Sheffield Church Burgesses*,
...to *Sheffield Grammar School*, ...to *Trustees of Birley's Charity*, ...to *Trustees of Wakefield & Sheffield Turnpike Trusts*, & Agent to the *Mentor Life Assurance Office.*

1883 – John James Wheat – Solicitor.
1905 – John James Wheat – Solicitor.
John Bristowe Wheat M.A. – Solicitor.
1920 – John Bristowe Wheat M.A. - Solicitor
1973 – 8 &10 Robert B. Grayson & Sons – Solicitors, commissioned for oaths.
Peter S. Wileman, L.L.D. – Solicitor.
2008 – 4 to 12 – Graysons – Solicitors.

Number 10.

Directories:
1854 – Henry Broomhead Sen. Esq.
1883 – Samuel Lockwood Levick – Accountant
James Hall – Architect etc., & Secretary *Fitzwilliam Permanent Benefit Building Society.*
British Workman's Assurance Co. Limited – John William Drake, Supt.
1905 – Joseph Arthur Darwent – Accountant.
Sheffield and District Confectioners Association – J. A. Darwent, Sec.
Wells, Epsom & Co. - Tea merchants.
Mark Woolman – Tailor.
1920 – Hall & Fenton – Architects, surveyors and Engineers.
1973 – 8 &10 Robert B. Grayson & Sons – Solicitors, comm.. for oaths..
Peter S. Wileman, L.L.D. – Solicitor.
2008 – 4 to 12 – Graysons – Solicitors.

Number 12.

Directories:
1854 – McDonald & Munroe – Linen & woollen drapers.
1883 – John Townend & Son – Land agents.
George R. Townend – Cutlery manufacturer.
1905 – William Edgar Ryves – Surgeon.
1920 – William Edgar Ryves L.R.C.P. & S. Edin. – Surgeon.

1973 –12 & 20 Slater,Elliott,Todd, Cooper & Co. – Solicitors, comm. for oaths.
2008 – 4 to 12 – Graysons – Solicitors.

Crossing back into the main Square:

Number 14 – After the Great War, ex servicemen formed associations to cater for welfare and comradely. One of these was the National Federation of Discharges and Demobilised Sailors and Soldiers. At a service held for the Roman Catholic men who had lost their lives from the St Vincent's Parish of Sheffield.

photo: Albert Jackson

Number 14

79

Over 2,000 ex servicemen accompanied by two bands marched through the town to a special Mass at the St Vincent's Church setting off from the Square.

The branch was amalgamated into the Royal British Legion when it opened at Lee Croft.

Number 14 and 16 are currently occupied by solicitors Lewis Francis Blackburn. Their partner; Kevin Excell, is the longest serving solicitor in the Square having practised here since 1972.

Blackburn & Co. moved the Square in 1939, occupying number 14, and then following a merger moved into number 16, now after an amalgamation with Lewis Francis to the practice, in the current form they have both buildings.

Little exists of the original building apart from its façade, like many others in the Square the *Health & Safety* regulations have seen the virtual rebuilding of the interiors.

Directories:
1854 – John Fisher – Glass and china dealer.
1883 – John Fisher – Glass and china dealer.
1905 – Fisher & Co. – Glass & china dealers.
1920 – National Federation of Discharged & Demobilised Sailors & Soldiers
              J. H. Firth, Sec.
1973 – Blackburn & Co. – Solicitors.
2008 – 14 & 16 – Lewis, Francis Blackburn – Solicitors.

Number 16 – For a century the premises played host as a printers. The ground floor had lost its original house frontage, like most of the properties during the nineteenth century in exchange for workshop / shop frontage, (much like the frontage of number 17).

Directories:
1854 – George Nicholson – Taylor, woollen draper and paletot maker.
1883 – Hall & Co., - Printers etc.
1905 – Arundel Printing Co. Ltd. - Printers
1920 – Arundel Printing Co. Ltd. – Printers.
1973 – Watson, Esam & Co. - Solicitors
2008 – 14 & 16 – Lewis, Francis Blackburn – Solicitors.

Number 18 – This is the Sheffield address known to more people than any other. Throughout the history of the Square it has been uppermost in the attention of visitors and correspondents.

photo: Albert Jackson

Number 18

As its first occupant, the upper floor was entered from a stone staircase, which protruded eighteen feet (5.75m) straight ahead into the Square. The top of this staircase was the point where the speaker addressed all the onlookers at political, religious and any other meeting.

It was the home initially of a Masonic Lodge, while the floor below was occupied as a store.

The Lodge moved away to the Wicker and the room let to the Johannes Chapel; they also used the room as a schoolroom.

Edward Hebblethwaite set up his academy here in 1811 And remained until 1865, then along with Number 20, it became the Middle Class School for Boys and Girls, a successful Fee paying school which prospered until the 1920's, when the aftermath of the Great War made it uneconomic and closed.

The next phase in its progression was to become a printworks and store until in the 1960's a redevelopment of a number of buildings took place to move away from the workshop and shop frontages and to revive its original appearance.

Number 18, along with number 26 were gutted and restored externally to their former appearance while internally they were rebuilt to the then modern status. The existing brick was reused at number 18, while the other building had new brick of a similar likeness.

These rebuilds were used as a theme by the Sheffield Architects (R.I.B.A) for their Conference, highlighting Sheffield's lead in this particular field.

After the refurbishment it was named 'Fanum House' and became the headquarters of the Automobile Association. At the end of their lease they moved to nearby St James Row.

Watson Esam solicitors had been in Bank Street until they were bombed out in the Sheffield Blitz of 1940.

They operated from an office in Broomhall until they were able to move back into the Square in 1964, when they moved into number 16.

They had a strong Quaker belief and during the war had observed a policy of not acting for companies dealing with munitions.

When number 18 became vacant they moved in and have expanded the business successfully from there.

Their commitment to charity and good causes has been a striking feature of the Company, Senior Partner Adam Pemberton, before his retirement in 2006 organised the Christmas Carol service that was held from the open window on the first floor since it was abandoned by Radio Sheffield.

courtesy of Sheffield Local History Library
The rebuilding of number 18

He still turns up for the concert with his Saxophone and enjoys keeping in touch with his colleagues and friends.

Directories:
1854 – Thomas Booker – Glass & china dealer.
      Edward Hebblethwaite - Academy
1883 – Henry Booker – Glass and china dealer.
1905 – 18 & 20 – Middle Class School for Boys, Girls & Infants
                  - Mr & Mrs Arthur Newell – principals.
1920 – 18 & 20 – Middle Class School for Boys, Girls & Infants
              Principal – James Longstaffe
1973 – Automobile Association – Motoring Association.
      D. Balfour & Sons. – Consulting Engineers.
2008 – Watson, Esam & Co. – Solicitors.

Number 20 – Doctor Booth was quite a noted surgeon, but is documented as the neighbour who complained about the pub next door having rats that were infesting the rest of the Square. He organised a petition of the Square for better behaviour.

The Sheffield Conservative Party had its headquarters for a time here before expanding to larger premises.

In a recent refurbishment remains of the Middle Class School was discovered.

photo; Albert Jackson

Number 20

Directories:
1854 – William Henry Booth - Surgeon
1883 – *Sheffield Conservative Club Ltd* – Evan Edward Liddell – Sec. Pro tem
      Borough of Sheffield Conservative & Constitutional Association
                        - Christopher Parrett, registration agent & sec.
1905 – 18 & 20 – Middle Class School for Boys, Girls & Infants
            - Mr & Mrs Arthur Newell – principals.

1920 – 18 & 20 – Middle Class School for Boys, Girls & Infants
                Principal – James Longstaffe.
1973 – 12 & 20 Slater,Elliott,Todd, Cooper & Co – Solicitors, comm. for oaths.
2008 – Cunningtons – Solicitors (To Let)

Number 22 – Best known as the Hebrew School, Saul Finkestine was Headmaster from its opening in the Square in

Design Consultants Liani Designs, took advantage of their occupation in the building by fitting it out in their style as a showroom. A relic of this was a spiral staircase that remained intact until the building refurbishment in 2003, when it was removed.

At the refurbishment, school books were discovered and 'graffiti' drawn onto the window ledges and fireplaces. The cellar still had the original sink and carcass.

photo: Albert Jackson 2003
The cellar of number 22

Directories:
1854 – William Henry Claytron – Auctioneer.
        John Hattersley – Furniture broker.
1883 – vacant
1905 – Sheffield Hebrew School – Saul Harry Finklestine, Headmaster.
1920 – Sheffield Hebrew School – Saul Harry Finklestine, Headmaster.
1973 – ***Paradise Buildings –***
        Liani Designs – Design consultant.
        Fulwood Estate Agents & Insurance Brokers – Est. agent, Ins. Brks.

85

W. Bunting Ltd – Check trader.
E. W. Hooper F.R.I.B.A. – Architect.
E.A. U. Ward & Co. – Engineers sales.
Leeds Diocesan Rescue – Protection and Child Welfare Society.
Catholic Rescue Society – Rescue Society.
2008 – Vacant

photo: Albert Jackson
Bootscraper outside number 22

Number 24 – Where Sir Francis Chantry set up in business as a commercial artist. He advertised in the Iris for sitters at just a few guineas. From here he moved to London to become a famous sculptor.

While in London he had commissions which included Royalty and the rich and famous. He has works of sculpture in many Cathedrals, his most well known figure being known as the 'Sleeping Children' in Lichfield Cathedral.

He maintained an address in Norfolk Row while progressing his career in London.

After his death he was buried at Norton Church, close to his birthplace.

86

From its period as a Commercial Stationers and legal Bookshop, it has now become, along with number 26, Barristers Chambers.

Directories:
1854 – William Cliff – Beer retailer.
1883 – John Johnson – Insurance Agent.
1905 – Thomas Warde – Bookseller.
1920 – Thomas Warde – Bookseller.
1973 – vacant
2008 – 24 & 26 – Paradise Chambers – Barristers Chambers.

photo: Albert Jackson
Number 26

Number 26 – The building, along with number 18, received a complete makeover in the 1960's. It is now along with number 24, Barristers Chambers.

Directories:
1854 –   James Neild – General furniture and tool broker, roman cement &
                   plaster of Paris depot.
1883 –   vacant
1905 –   W. Hattersley & Co. - Merchants
1920 –   Haydn A. Morley – Solicitor.
           J. H. Horner – Accountant.
           Theophilus Sievewright – Law Stationer.
           Charles E. V. Hall – Mechanical engineer.
1973 –   vacant
2008 –   24 & 26 – Paradise Chambers – Barristers Chambers.

There is another legend attached to the Square of a solicitor who visited the local pubs and *enjoyed* his drink. He arrived in the Square in the morning on horseback, tethering it to the downpipe outside his office. On at least one occasion, his horse broke loose and had to be *'rounded up'*.

Illustration: Dennis Dalby

88

Appendix

Charles (Charlie) Edward Peace

Charles Edward Peace was a clever young chap, as would be discovered in later life, however at school he paid more attention to what was happening outside and concluded that he would make his mark on the world without education.

Leaving Hebblethwaite's Academy in 1844, when he was just 12 years old, he took a job at the Millsand's steelworks as an apprentice.

On his thirteenth birthday he was badly injured by a red hot steel bar piercing his thigh and was hospitalised for eighteen months and declared disabled.

He then turned to crime, spending much of his teens in prison. He was a master of disguise and much of his criminal activities were done in disguise.

While in prison about he had picked up a knowledge of music and when he was released he had become quite proficient and was able to earn cash and drink by travelling around Inns playing his violin.

He had married a woman from Bradford and after a prison sentence, they returned to Sheffield where they settled down in Darnall.

Next door their neighbour's, Mr & Mrs Dyson had recently arrived from America with their five year old son. Charlie took a shine for Catherine Dyson and began a relationship with her, taking her to local public

After a while she ended the affair but Charlie did not accept this and began to pester her.

After threatening both Catherine and her husband with a pistol, Charlie and his wife fled Sheffield staying in Hull and Manchester. It was while in Manchester that he shot dead a policeman who disturbed him in a robbery.

Later the Dyson's spotted a woman watching their house and suspected that this was Charlie in disguise and moved home to Banner Cross. Charlie found out where they were and on 29th November 1876, he went there and threatened both of them again, this time after a struggle he killed Arthur Dyson with his second shot.

Making his getaway, he was arrested almost two years later while being disturbed in a house-burglary in London after firing shots at the Police.

He was charged and committed for trial in an alias name but his true identity was discovered and after receiving a life sentence he was sent back to Sheffield to stand trial for the Arthur Dyson murder.

On the journey back Charlie, despite being manacled, threw himself off the train, leaving a note requesting that he be buried in Darnall.

He survived and after standing before the Sheffield Magistrate was committed for trial at Leeds Assizes.

He was found guilty of the murder of Catherine Dyson and also of the Manchester policeman and sentenced to be hanged.

His execution took place at Armley gaol, Leeds on February 25th 1879. He went to the gallows after speaking to the witnesses present and as he prepared for death he bade Hangman Marwood; 'Good bye and God bless you'.

Outside a crowd of 1,000 were waiting in the icy cold morning to see the black flag of death hoisted on the flagpole.